LON

RAILWAY ATLAS

Joe Brown

Ian Allan
PUBLISHING

First published 2015

ISBN 978 0 7110 3818 9

Published by Ian Allan Publishing

an imprint of Ian Allan Publishing Ltd, Hersham, Surrey KT12 4RG.
Printed in Wales

Visit the Ian Allan Publishing website at www.ianallanpublishing.com

Front cover:
With The Shard and Guys Hospital in the background, Class 465/1 Networker No 465196 approaches Waterloo East on 1 March 2012, forming the 14.24 Southeastern service from Gillingham to Charing Cross, via Woolwich Arsenal.
Brian Morrison

Preface to the First Edition

This book is designed to complement my fourth edition of the *London Railway Atlas* (Ian Allan) in a portable, pocket-sized format in the long tradition of the 'abc' titles.

In terms of coverage, this title covers the entire London Underground system and the majority of the National Rail system within the Greater London area. Where branch lines terminated just outside of the area covered, I have included the termini on insets. As the atlas is to scale, unfortunately with the best will in the world this manipulation is required, and some outer areas of London have had to be excluded.

The atlas depicts every line past and present, including goods and industrial routes, and every passenger station past and present is depicted and named. Depots / sidings and goods / industrial facilities are shown but not named, and similarly dates in the Index refer to the passenger stations only. Producing the book has been a relatively straightforward exercise of removing the wealth of detail from the *London Railway Atlas* and depicting routes and stations in a far more simplistic format.

I hope that this book would be a field companion giving the overview, while the fourth edition of the *London Railway Atlas* provides the comprehensive detail.

Please feel free to email me with any feedback or further information at:

atlasupdate@blueyonder.co.uk

Joe Brown, London, January 2015

Abbreviations

CLR	Central London Railway
CSLR	City & South London Railway
CTL	Croydon Tramlink
DLR	Docklands Light Railway
ECR	Eastern Counties Railway
ELR	East London Railway
EWIDBJR	East & West India Docks & Birmingham Junction Railway
GCC	Gaslight & Coke Company
GCR	Great Central Railway
GER	Great Eastern Railway
GNR	Great Northern Railway
GWR	Great Western Railway
LBLR	London & Blackwall Railway
LBSCR	London, Brighton & South Coast Railway
LCDR	London, Chatham & Dover Railway
LMS	London, Midland & Scottish Railway
LNER	London & North Eastern Railway
LNWR	London & North Western Railway
LPTB	London Passenger Transport Board
LSWR	London & South Western Railway
LTE	London Transport Executive
LUL	London Underground Ltd
MDR	Metropolitan District Railway
MER	Millwall Extension Railway
MET	Metropolitan Railway
MHPR	Muswell Hill & Palace Railway
MID	Midland Railway
MKR	Mid Kent Railway
MSJWR	Metropolitan & St John's Wood Railway
NLR	North London Railway
NR	Network Rail
SER	South Eastern Railway
TfL	Transport for London
UERL	Underground Electric Railways of London
WELCPR	West End of London & Crystal Palace Railway
WLER	West London Extension Railway
WLR	West London Railway

Explanation of Map Symbols

● Station (open)	
○ Station (built but did not open)	
★ Depot / carriage sidings / engine shed (open)	
┊ Tunnel	Line Open
▲ Goods facility (e.g aggregates, waste, scrap, oil) (open)	
■ Works / factory (open)	
Ⓤ Station (under construction)	Line under construction or proposed
Ⓟ Station (proposed)	
○ Station (closed)	
☆ Depot / carriage sidings / engine shed (closed)	
Tunnel (closed)	Line Closed
△ Goods facility (closed)	
□ Works / factory (closed)	

Network Rail	LUL Jubilee Line
LUL Bakerloo Line	LUL Northern Line
LUL Central Line	LUL Piccadilly Line
LUL Victoria Line	LUL Waterloo & City Line
LUL Metropolitan Line	Docklands Light Railway
LUL District Line	London Tramlink Croydon
LUL Circle Line	Preserved Railways
LUL Hammersmith & City Line	

Diagram of Maps

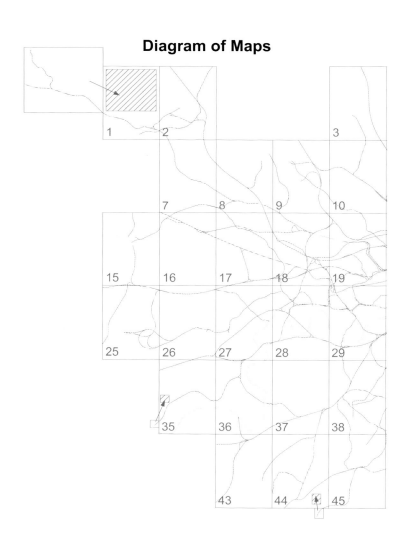

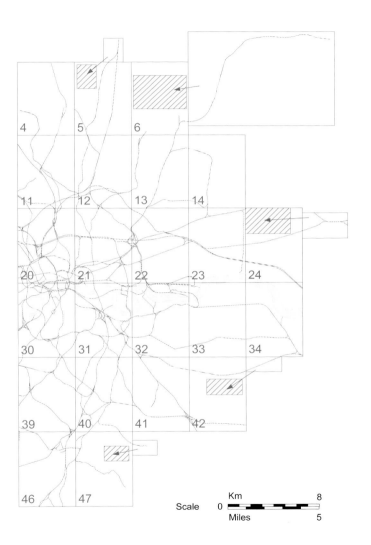

4	5	6
11	12	13	14
20	21	22	23	24
30	31	32	33	34
39	40	41	42
46	47

Scale 0 Km 8

Miles 5

Chesham

Amersham

△ Chalfont & Latimer

2

Continuation (not to same scale)

Chorleywood

★ △ ★

Rickmansworth

△

○

Rickmansworth (Church Street)

1

Scale

Km 0.5 1 1.5 2
0

Miles ¼ ½ ¾ 1

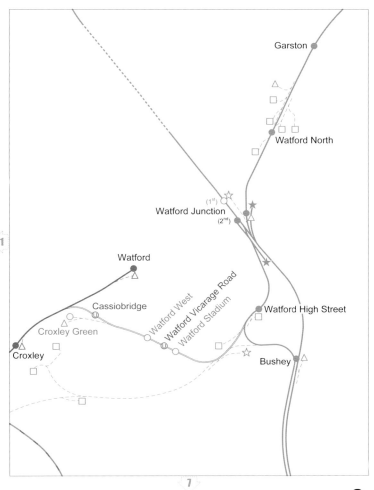

Scale

Km 0   0.5   1   1.5   2

Miles ¼   ½   ¾   1

2

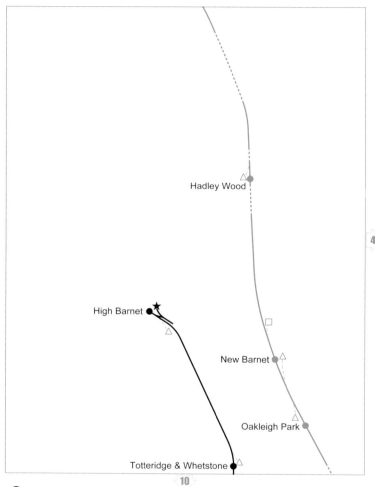

Hadley Wood

High Barnet

New Barnet

Oakleigh Park

Totteridge & Whetstone

3

Scale

Km 0.5 1 1.5 2

0

Miles ¼ ½ ¾ 1

4

10

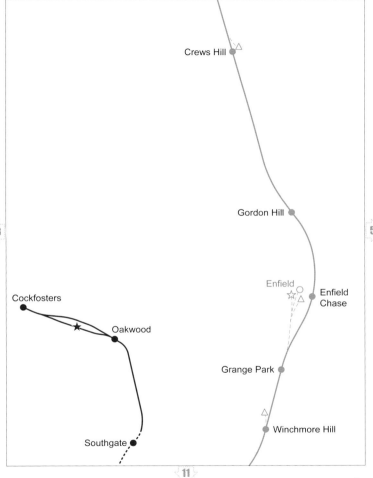

Crews Hill

Gordon Hill

Enfield

Enfield
Chase

Cockfosters

Oakwood

Grange Park

Southgate

Winchmore Hill

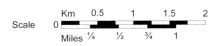

Scale

Km 0.5 1 1.5 2
0
Miles ¼ ½ ¾ 1

4

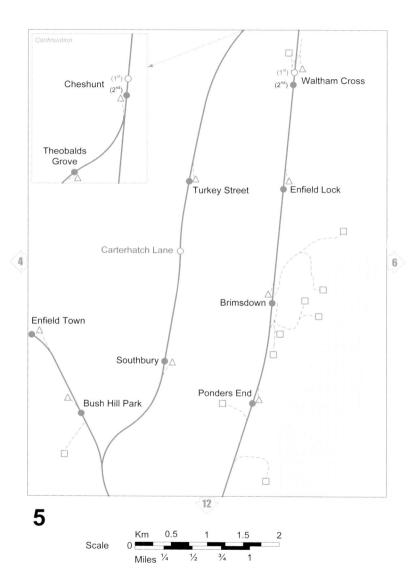

Continuation

Cheshunt (1st) (2nd)

Theobalds Grove

Waltham Cross (1st) (2nd)

Turkey Street

Enfield Lock

Carterhatch Lane

Brimsdown

Enfield Town

Southbury

Bush Hill Park

Ponders End

4

6

12

5

Scale

Km 0.5 1 1.5 2
0

Miles ¼ ½ ¾ 1

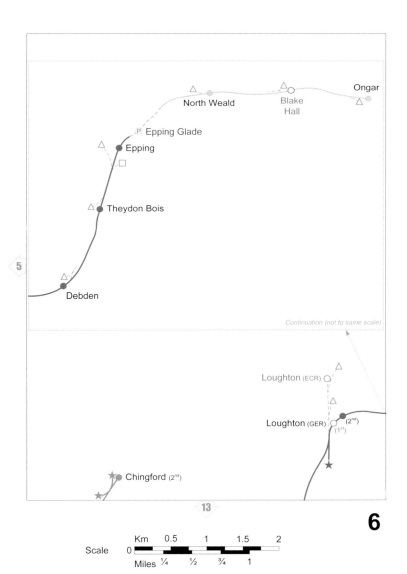

Ongar

Blake Hall

North Weald

Epping Glade

Epping

Theydon Bois

Debden

Continuation (not to same scale)

Loughton (ECR)

Loughton (GER)

(1st) (2nd)

Chingford (2nd)

6

Scale

Km 0.5 1 1.5 2
0

Miles ¼ ½ ¾ 1

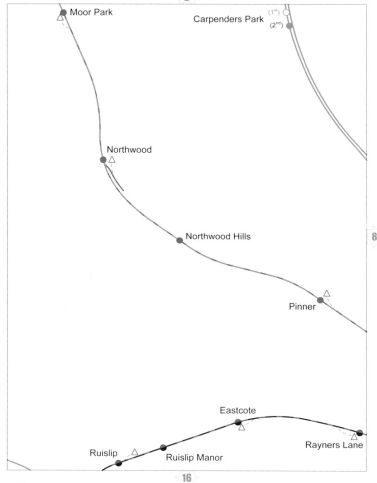

7

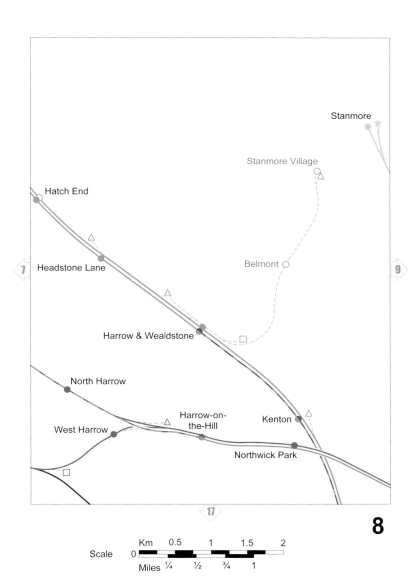

Stanmore

Stanmore Village

Hatch End

Headstone Lane

Belmont

7

9

Harrow & Wealdstone

North Harrow

Harrow-on-
the-Hill

Kenton

West Harrow

Northwick Park

17

8

Scale

Km   0.5   1   1.5   2

0

Miles ¼   ½   ¾   1

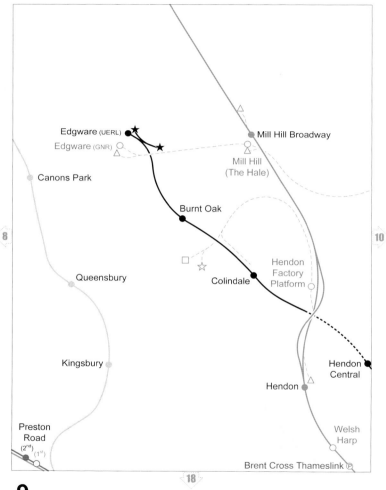

Edgware (UERL)

Edgware (GNR)

Mill Hill Broadway

Canons Park

Mill Hill
(The Hale)

Burnt Oak

8

10

Hendon
Factory
Platform

Queensbury

Colindale

Kingsbury

Hendon
Central

Hendon

Preston
Road
(2nd) (1st)

Welsh
Harp

Brent Cross Thameslink Ⓟ

18

9

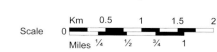

Scale

Km   0.5   1   1.5   2

0

Miles ¼   ½   ¾   1

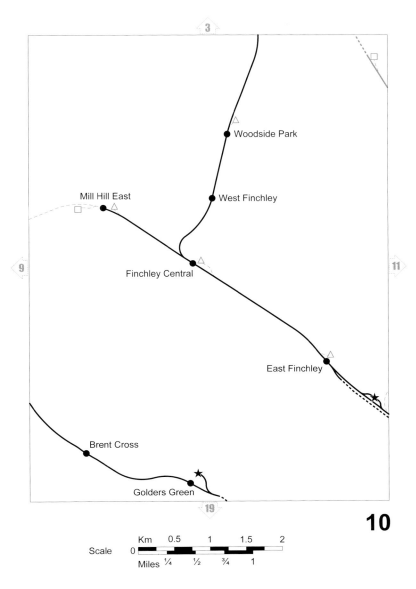

Woodside Park

Mill Hill East

West Finchley

Finchley Central

East Finchley

Brent Cross

Golders Green

3

9

11

19

10

Scale

Km 0.5 1 1.5 2
0
Miles ¼ ½ ¾ 1

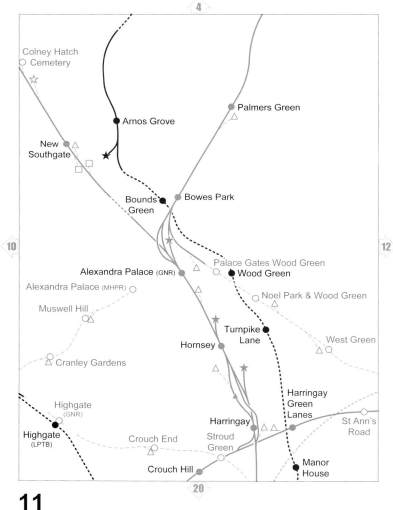

Colney Hatch Cemetery

Palmers Green

Arnos Grove

New Southgate

Bounds Green

Bowes Park

Alexandra Palace (GNR)

Palace Gates Wood Green

Wood Green

Alexandra Palace (MHPR)

Noel Park & Wood Green

Muswell Hill

Turnpike Lane

West Green

Hornsey

Cranley Gardens

Highgate (GNR)

Harringay Green Lanes

Highgate (LPTB)

Harringay

St Ann's Road

Crouch End

Stroud Green

Manor House

Crouch Hill

11

Scale

Km   0.5   1   1.5   2

0

Miles   ¼   ½   ¾   1

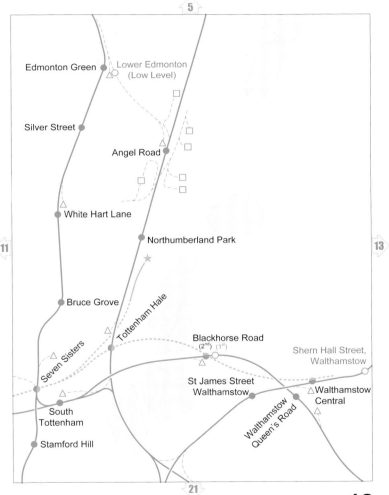

Edmonton Green
Lower Edmonton
(Low Level)

Silver Street

Angel Road

White Hart Lane

Northumberland Park

Bruce Grove

Tottenham Hale

Seven Sisters

Blackhorse Road
(2nd) (1st)

Shern Hall Street,
Walthamstow

St James Street
Walthamstow

South
Tottenham

Walthamstow
Queen's Road

Walthamstow
Central

Stamford Hill

12

| Scale | Km 0 | 0.5 | 1 | 1.5 | 2 |

Miles ¼ ½ ¾ 1

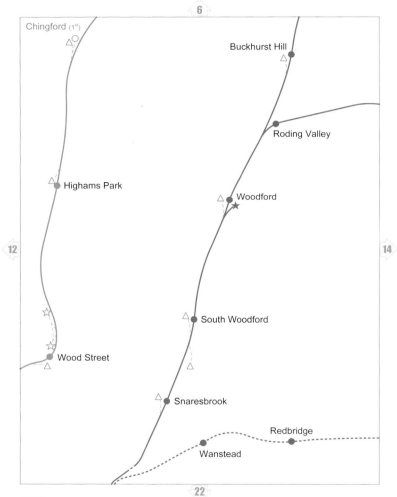

Chingford (1st)

Buckhurst Hill

Roding Valley

Highams Park

Woodford

South Woodford

Wood Street

Snaresbrook

Redbridge

Wanstead

13

Scale

Km 0.5 1 1.5 2
0

Miles ¼ ½ ¾ 1

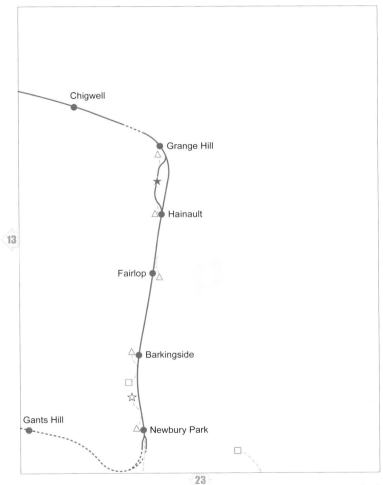

Chigwell

Grange Hill

Hainault

Fairlop

Barkingside

Gants Hill

Newbury Park

Scale

Km 0.5 1 1.5 2

0

Miles ¼ ½ ¾ 1

14

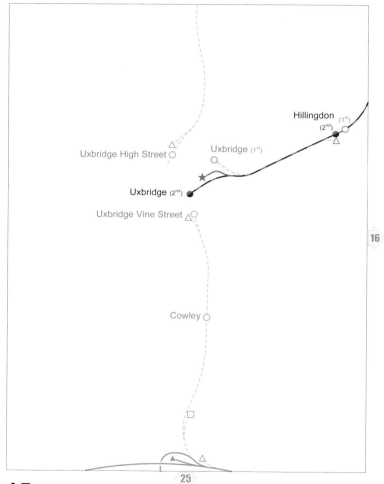

Hillingdon (1st)

(2nd)

Uxbridge (1st)

Uxbridge High Street

Uxbridge (2nd)

Uxbridge Vine Street

Cowley

16

25

15

Scale

Km 0.5 1 1.5 2

0

Miles ¼ ½ ¾ 1

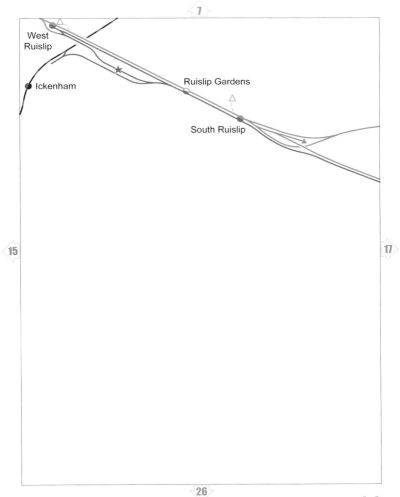

West
Ruislip

Ickenham

Ruislip Gardens

South Ruislip

16

Scale

Km   0.5   1   1.5   2
0
Miles ¼   ½   ¾   1

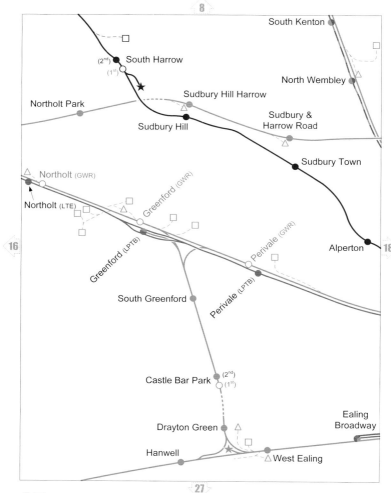

South Kenton

South Harrow
(2ⁿᵈ)
(1ˢᵗ)

Sudbury Hill Harrow

North Wembley

Northolt Park

Sudbury Hill

Sudbury & Harrow Road

Sudbury Town

Northolt (GWR)

Greenford (GWR)

Northolt (LTE)

Greenford (GWR)

Greenford (LPTB)

Perivale (GWR)

Perivale (LPTB)

Alperton

South Greenford

Castle Bar Park
(2ⁿᵈ)
(1ˢᵗ)

Ealing Broadway

Drayton Green

Hanwell

West Ealing

17

Scale

Km 0.5   1   1.5   2
0

Miles ¼   ½   ¾   1

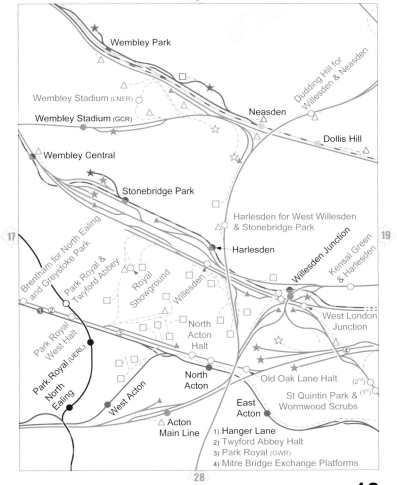

Wembley Park

Wembley Stadium (LNER)

Wembley Stadium (GCR)

Dudding Hill for Willesden & Neasden

Neasden

Dollis Hill

Wembley Central

Stonebridge Park

Harlesden for West Willesden & Stonebridge Park

Brentham for North Ealing and Greystoke Park

Park Royal & Twyford Abbey

Harlesden

Willesden Junction

Kensal Green & Harlesden

Royal Showground

Willesden

West London Junction

Park Royal West Halt

North Acton Halt

① ②

③

Park Royal (UERL)

North Ealing

Old Oak Lane Halt

St Quintin Park & (1st)
Wormwood Scrubs

(2nd)

④

West Acton

North Acton

East Acton

Acton Main Line

1) Hanger Lane
2) Twyford Abbey Halt
3) Park Royal (GWR)
4) Mitre Bridge Exchange Platforms

18

Scale

Km 0.5   1   1.5   2
0

Miles ¼   ½   ¾   1

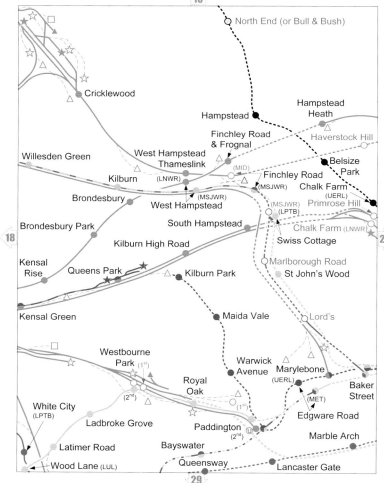

North End (or Bull & Bush)

Hampstead Heath

Hampstead

Haverstock Hill

Cricklewood

Finchley Road & Frognal

West Hampstead Thameslink

Belsize Park

Willesden Green

(MID)

Finchley Road

Kilburn

(LNWR)

(MSJWR)

Chalk Farm (UERL)

Brondesbury

West Hampstead (MSJWR)

(MSJWR) (LPTB)

Primrose Hill

Brondesbury Park

South Hampstead

Chalk Farm (LNWR)

18

Swiss Cottage

20

Kilburn High Road

Kensal Rise

Queens Park

Marlborough Road

Kilburn Park

St John's Wood

Kensal Green

Maida Vale

Lord's

Westbourne Park (1st)

Warwick Avenue

Marylebone (UERL)

(2nd)

Royal Oak

(MET)

Baker Street

White City (LPTB)

Edgware Road

Ladbroke Grove

(1st)

Latimer Road

Paddington (2nd)

Marble Arch

Wood Lane (LUL)

Bayswater

Queensway

Lancaster Gate

19

Scale

Km 0.5   1   1.5   2

0

Miles ¼   ½   ¾   1

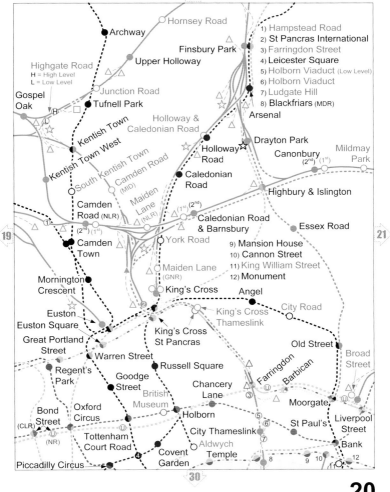

Archway

Hornsey Road

1) Hampstead Road
2) St Pancras International
3) Farringdon Street
4) Leicester Square
5) Holborn Viaduct (Low Level)
6) Holborn Viaduct
7) Ludgate Hill
8) Blackfriars (MDR)

Upper Holloway

Finsbury Park

Highgate Road
H = High Level
L = Low Level

Gospel Oak

H

Junction Road

Tufnell Park

Kentish Town

Kentish Town West

Holloway & Caledonian Road

Arsenal

Drayton Park

Holloway Road

Canonbury
(2nd) (1st)

Mildmay Park

South Kentish Town

Camden Road (MID)

Caledonian Road

Maiden Lane (NLR)

Camden Road (NLR)
(2nd) (1st)

(1st) (2nd)

Highbury & Islington

Caledonian Road & Barnsbury

Essex Road

Camden Town

York Road

9) Mansion House
10) Cannon Street
11) King William Street
12) Monument

Mornington Crescent

Maiden Lane (GNR)

King's Cross

Angel

City Road

Euston

King's Cross Thameslink

Euston Square

King's Cross St Pancras

Old Street

Great Portland Street

Warren Street

Russell Square

Farringdon

Barbican

Broad Street

Regent's Park

Goodge Street

British Museum

Chancery Lane

③

Moorgate

Bond Street
(CLR)

U
(NR)

Oxford Circus

Holborn

⑤
⑥

St Paul's

Liverpool Street

Tottenham Court Road

City Thameslink

⑦

Bank

Piccadilly Circus

④

Covent Garden

Aldwych

Temple

8

9 10

12

11

20

Scale

Km   0.5   1   1.5   2
0

Miles ¼   ½   ¾   1

19
21

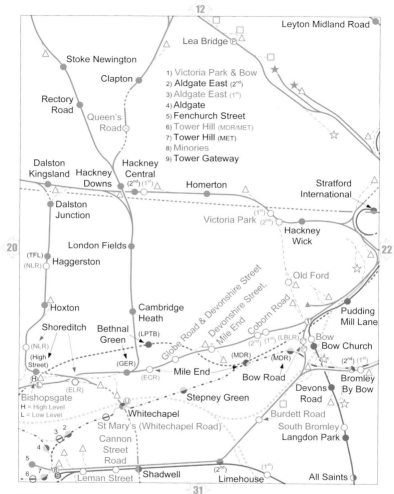

Leyton Midland Road

Lea Bridge

Stoke Newington

Clapton

1) Victoria Park & Bow
2) Aldgate East (2nd)
3) Aldgate East (1st)
4) Aldgate
5) Fenchurch Street
6) Tower Hill (MDR/MET)
7) Tower Hill (MET)
8) Minories
9) Tower Gateway

Rectory Road

Queen's Road

Dalston Kingsland

Hackney Downs

Hackney Central
(2nd) (1st)

Homerton

Stratford International

Dalston Junction

Victoria Park (1st)
(2nd)

Hackney Wick

London Fields

(TFL)
(NLR) Haggerston

Old Ford

Hoxton

Cambridge Heath

Globe Road & Devonshire Street,
Devonshire Street,
Mile End

Coborn Road

Pudding Mill Lane

Shoreditch

(NLR)

Bethnal Green
(LPTB)

(1st) (LBLR)

Bow
Bow Church

(High Street)

(GER)

(ECR)

Mile End

(MDR)

(MDR)

Bow Road

(2nd) (1st)

Bromley By Bow

Bishopsgate
H = High Level
L = Low Level

(ELR)

Stepney Green

Devons Road

Whitechapel

Burdett Road

3 2

St Mary's (Whitechapel Road)

South Bromley

4

Cannon Street Road

Langdon Park

5

6 7 8
9

Leman Street

Shadwell

(2nd) (1st)

Limehouse

All Saints

21

Scale

Km   0.5   1   1.5   2
0

Miles ¼   ½   ¾   1

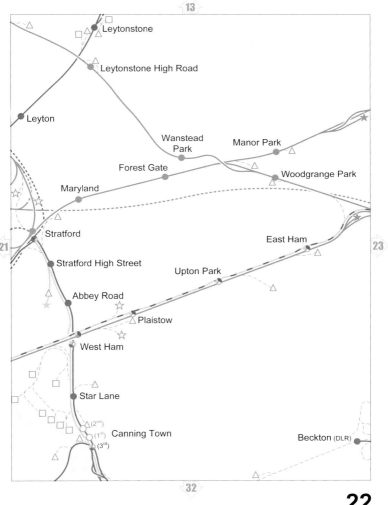

Leytonstone

Leytonstone High Road

Leyton

Wanstead Park

Manor Park

Forest Gate

Woodgrange Park

Maryland

Stratford

East Ham

Stratford High Street

Upton Park

Abbey Road

Plaistow

West Ham

Star Lane

(2nd)
(1st) Canning Town
(3rd)

Beckton (DLR)

22

Scale

Km 0.5 1 1.5 2
0
Miles ¼ ½ ¾ 1

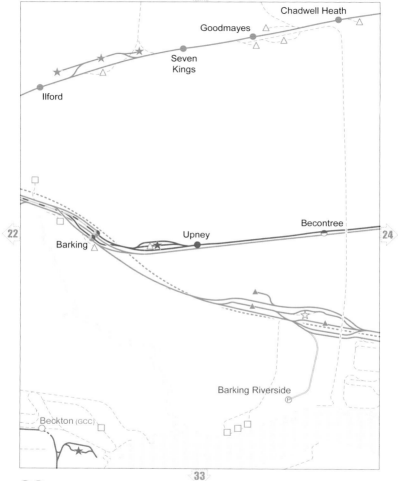

Chadwell Heath

Goodmayes

Seven
Kings

Ilford

Barking

Upney

Becontree

Barking Riverside

Beckton (GCC)

23

Scale Km 0.5 1 1.5 2

0

Miles ¼ ½ ¾ 1

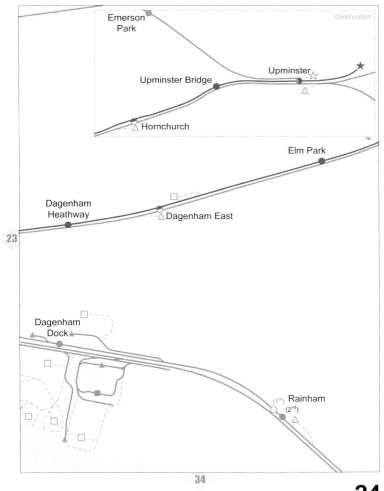

Emerson Park

Upminster

Upminster Bridge

Hornchurch

Elm Park

Dagenham Heathway

Dagenham East

23

Dagenham Dock

Rainham
(1st)
(2nd)

34

24

Scale

Km 0.5 1 1.5 2
0

Miles ¼ ½ ¾ 1

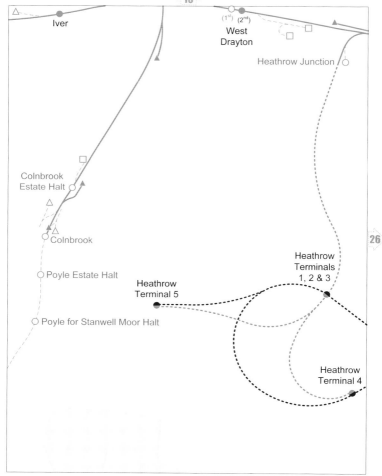

Iver

West Drayton
(1st) (2nd)

Heathrow Junction

Colnbrook
Estate Halt

Colnbrook

Poyle Estate Halt

Heathrow
Terminals
1, 2 & 3

Heathrow
Terminal 5

Poyle for Stanwell Moor Halt

Heathrow
Terminal 4

25

Scale

Km 0.5   1   1.5   2
0

Miles ¼   ½   ¾   1

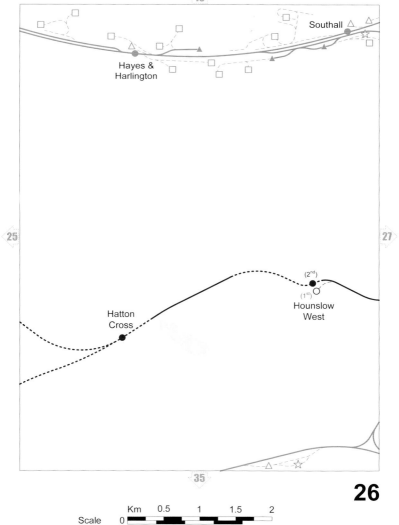

Southall

Hayes &
Harlington

25   27

(2nd)

(1st)

Hounslow
West

Hatton
Cross

35

26

Scale   Km   0.5   1   1.5   2
0
Miles   ¼   ½   ¾   1

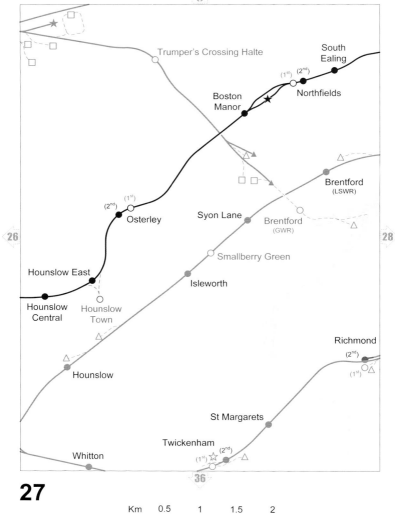

Trumper's Crossing Halte

South
Ealing

(1st) (2nd)

Boston
Manor

Northfields

Brentford
(LSWR)

(2nd) (1st)

Osterley

Syon Lane

Brentford
(GWR)

Hounslow East

Smallberry Green

Hounslow
Central

Isleworth

Hounslow
Town

Richmond

(2nd)
(1st)

Hounslow

St Margarets

Whitton

Twickenham

(1st) (2nd)

27

Scale

Km   0.5   1   1.5   2

0

Miles ¼   ½   ¾   1

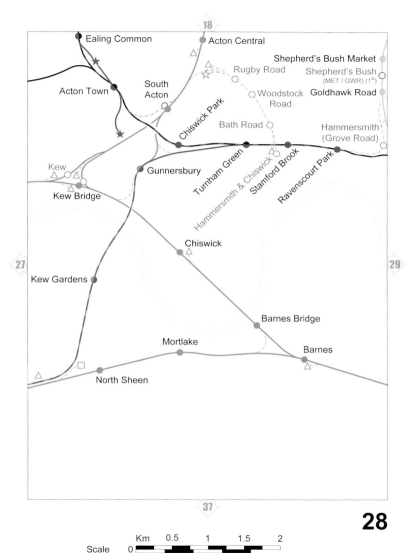

Ealing Common
Acton Central
Shepherd's Bush Market
Shepherd's Bush
(MET / GWR) (1st)
Rugby Road
Acton Town
South
Acton
Goldhawk Road
Woodstock
Road
Chiswick Park
Bath Road
Hammersmith
(Grove Road)
Turnham Green
Gunnersbury
Hammersmith & Chiswick
Stamford Brook
Ravenscourt Park
Kew
Kew Bridge
Chiswick

Kew Gardens
Barnes Bridge
Mortlake
Barnes
North Sheen

28

Km 0.5 1 1.5 2
Scale 0
Miles ¼ ½ ¾ 1

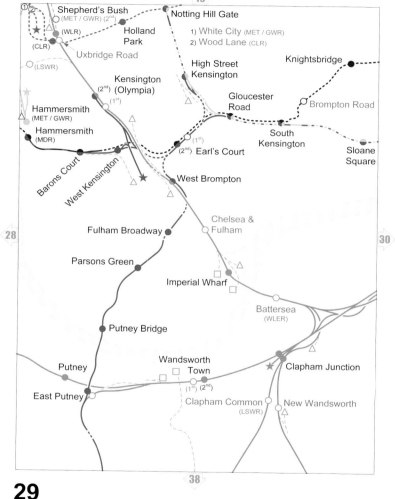

29

Scale

| Km | 0.5 | 1 | 1.5 | 2 |

Miles ¼ ½ ¾ 1

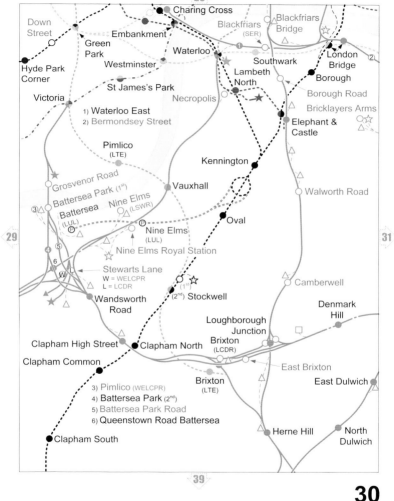

20

Down Street

Green Park

Embankment

Charing Cross

Blackfriars (SER)

Blackfriars Bridge

Hyde Park Corner

Waterloo

Westminster

Southwark

London Bridge

Victoria

St James's Park

Lambeth North

Borough

1) Waterloo East
2) Bermondsey Street

Necropolis

Borough Road

Bricklayers Arms

Pimlico (LTE)

Elephant & Castle

Grosvenor Road

Kennington

Battersea Park (1st)

Vauxhall

Walworth Road

Battersea (LUL)

Nine Elms (LSWR)

29

Nine Elms (LUL)

Oval

31

Nine Elms Royal Station

Stewarts Lane
W = WELCPR
L = LCDR

Camberwell

Wandsworth Road

(1st)
(2nd) Stockwell

Denmark Hill

Clapham High Street

Clapham North

Loughborough Junction

Brixton (LCDR)

East Brixton

Clapham Common

Brixton (LTE)

East Dulwich

3) Pimlico (WELCPR)
4) Battersea Park (2nd)
5) Battersea Park Road
6) Queenstown Road Battersea

Clapham South

Herne Hill

North Dulwich

39

30

Scale
Km 0 0.5 1 1.5 2
Miles ¼ ½ ¾ 1

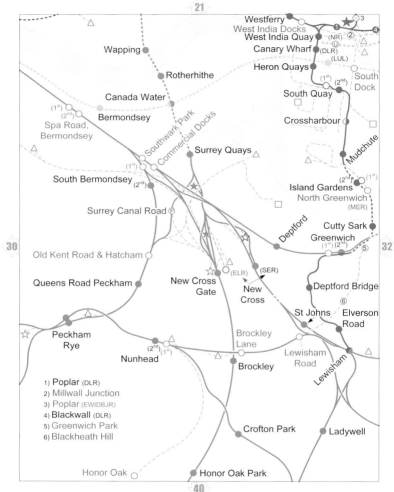

Westferry
West India Docks
West India Quay
Canary Wharf
(NR)
(DLR)
(LUL)
Heron Quays
South Dock
(1st) (2nd)
South Quay
Crossharbour
Mudchute
Wapping
Rotherhithe
Canada Water
Bermondsey
(1st)
(2nd)
Spa Road, Bermondsey
Southwark Park
Commercial Docks
Surrey Quays
South Bermondsey
(1st)
(2nd)
Surrey Canal Road ℗
Old Kent Road & Hatcham
Queens Road Peckham
New Cross Gate
(ELR)
(SER)
New Cross
Deptford
Island Gardens
North Greenwich
(2nd) (1st)
(MER)
Cutty Sark
Greenwich
(1st) (2nd)
5
Deptford Bridge
6
St Johns
Elverson Road
Brockley Lane
Lewisham Road
Lewisham
Peckham Rye
Nunhead
(2nd) (1st)
Brockley
1) Poplar (DLR)
2) Millwall Junction
3) Poplar (EWIDBJR)
4) Blackwall (DLR)
5) Greenwich Park
6) Blackheath Hill

Crofton Park
Ladywell

Honor Oak
Honor Oak Park

31

Scale
Km 0   0.5   1   1.5   2
Miles ¼   ½   ¾   1

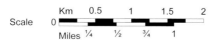

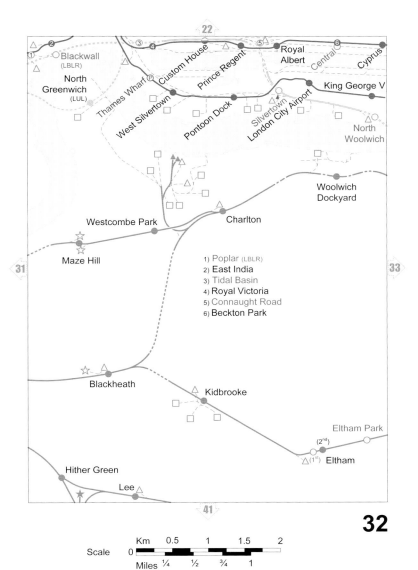

Blackwall
(LBLR)

North
Greenwich
(LUL)

East India
Poplar (LBLR)

Thames Wharf

Custom House

West Silvertown

Prince Regent

Royal
Albert

Central

Cyprus

King George V

Pontoon Dock

Silvertown

London City Airport

North
Woolwich

Woolwich
Dockyard

Westcombe Park

Charlton

Maze Hill

1) Poplar (LBLR)
2) East India
3) Tidal Basin
4) Royal Victoria
5) Connaught Road
6) Beckton Park

Blackheath

Kidbrooke

Eltham Park

(2nd)

(1st) Eltham

Hither Green

Lee

32

Scale

Km 0 0.5 1 1.5 2

Miles ¼ ½ ¾ 1

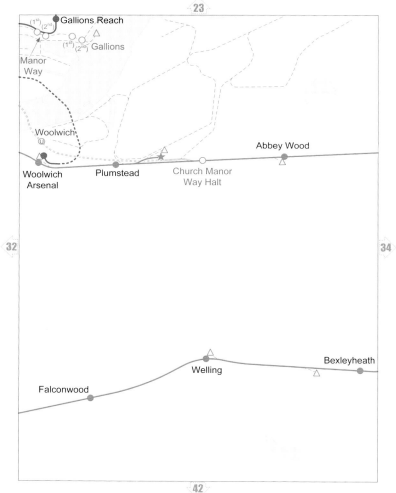

(1st) Gallions Reach
(2nd)

(1st) (2nd) Gallions

Manor
Way

Woolwich
Ⓤ

Abbey Wood

Woolwich
Arsenal

Plumstead

Church Manor
Way Halt

Welling

Bexleyheath

Falconwood

33

Scale

Km   0.5   1   1.5   2
0

Miles ¼   ½   ¾   1

Belvedere

Erith

Slade Green

Barnehurst

Continued on page 42 inset

34

Scale

| Km | 0.5 | 1 | 1.5 | 2 |

0

Miles ¼ ½ ¾ 1

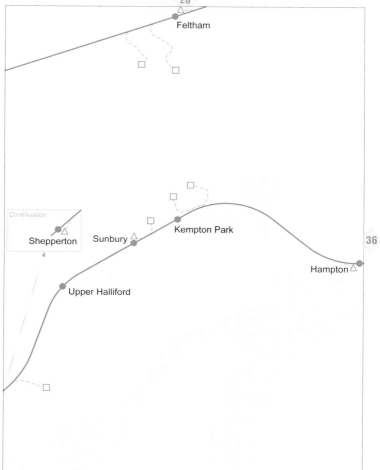

Feltham

Continuation

Shepperton

Sunbury

Kempton Park

Hampton

Upper Halliford

35

Scale

Km 0.5 1 1.5 2

0

Miles ¼ ½ ¾ 1

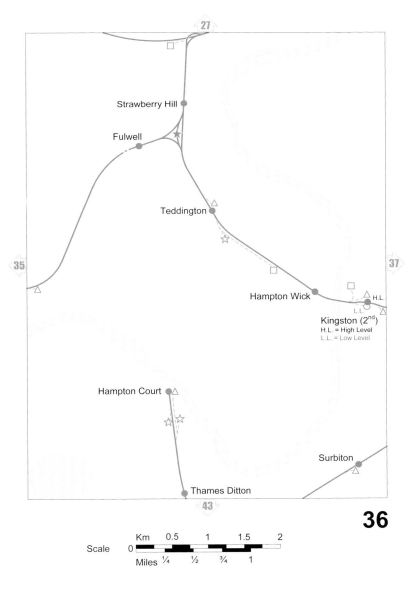

Strawberry Hill

Fulwell

Teddington

Hampton Wick

Kingston (2nd)
H.L. = High Level
L.L. = Low Level

H.L.
L.L.

Hampton Court

Surbiton

Thames Ditton

36

Scale

| Km | 0.5 | 1 | 1.5 | 2 |

| Miles | ¼ | ½ | ¾ | 1 |

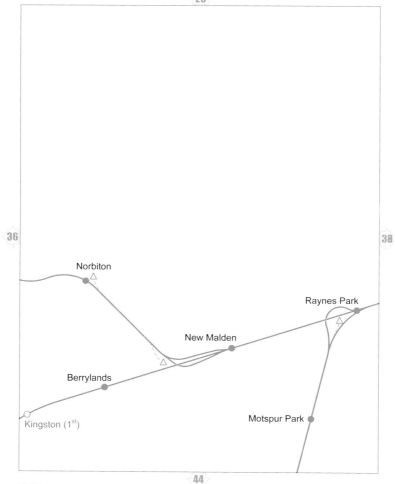

28

36

38

Norbiton

Raynes Park

New Malden

Berrylands

Motspur Park

Kingston (1ˢᵗ)

44

37

Scale
Km   0.5   1   1.5   2
0
Miles   ¼   ½   ¾   1

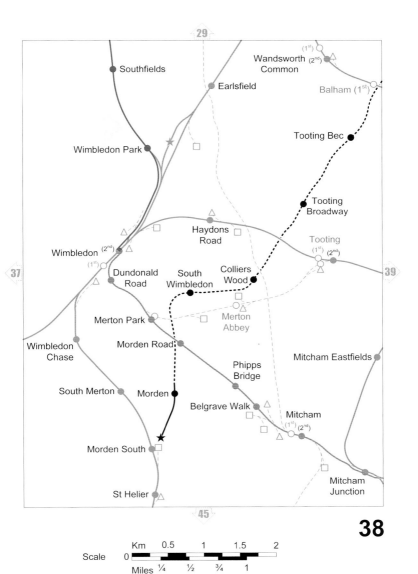

Southfields

Earlsfield

Wandsworth Common (2nd) (1st)

Balham (1st)

Tooting Bec

Wimbledon Park

Tooting Broadway

Haydons Road

Tooting (1st) (2nd)

Wimbledon (2nd)
(1st)

Dundonald Road

South Wimbledon

Colliers Wood

Merton Park

Merton Abbey

Wimbledon Chase

Morden Road

Mitcham Eastfields

Phipps Bridge

South Merton

Morden

Belgrave Walk

Mitcham (1st) (2nd)

Morden South

Mitcham Junction

St Helier

38

Scale

Km 0.5 1 1.5 2

0

Miles ¼ ½ ¾ 1

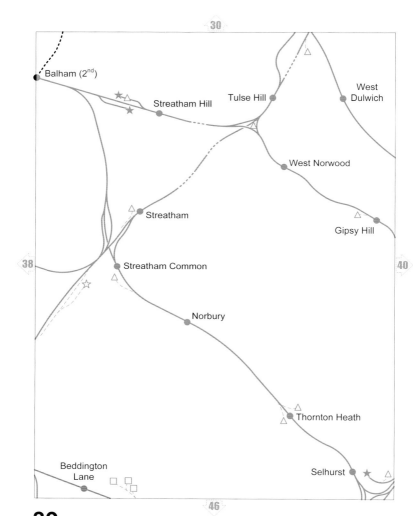

Balham (2nd)

Streatham Hill

Tulse Hill

West Dulwich

West Norwood

Streatham

Gipsy Hill

Streatham Common

Norbury

Thornton Heath

Beddington Lane

Selhurst

39

Scale

Km 0.5 1 1.5 2

0

Miles ¼ ½ ¾ 1

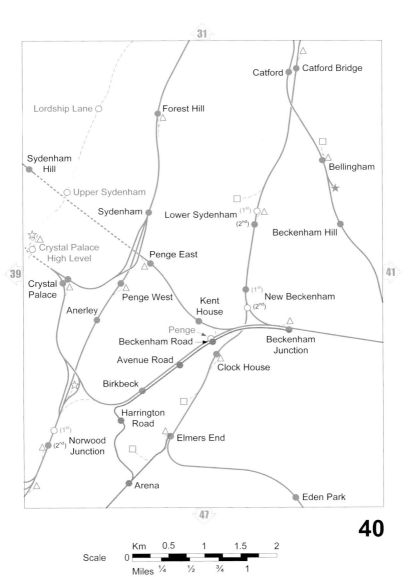

Lordship Lane ○

Catford ● ● Catford Bridge

Forest Hill △

Sydenham Hill ●

○ Upper Sydenham

Sydenham ●

Lower Sydenham (1st) ○ △
(2nd) ●

☆△
○ Crystal Palace High Level

◇ 39

Penge East ●
△

Crystal Palace ●
△

Anerley ●

Penge West △

Kent House ●

New Beckenham (1st)
○ (2nd)

Bellingham ●
□
△
★

Beckenham Hill ●

◇ 41

△

Penge ➤
Beckenham Road ○

Beckenham Junction △

Avenue Road ●
△

Birkbeck △
☆

Clock House ●

Harrington Road ●
□
△

Norwood Junction (1st) ○
△ (2nd)

Elmers End ●
□

Arena ●

Eden Park ●

◇ 31

◇ 47

40

Scale
Km 0   0.5   1   1.5   2
Miles ¼ ½ ¾ 1

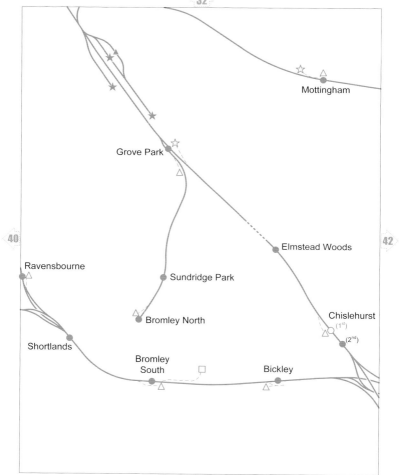

Mottingham

Grove Park

40

42

Elmstead Woods

Ravensbourne

Sundridge Park

Chislehurst
(1st)
(2nd)

Bromley North

Shortlands

Bromley
South

Bickley

41

Scale

Km   0.5   1   1.5   2
0
Miles ¼ ½ ¾ 1

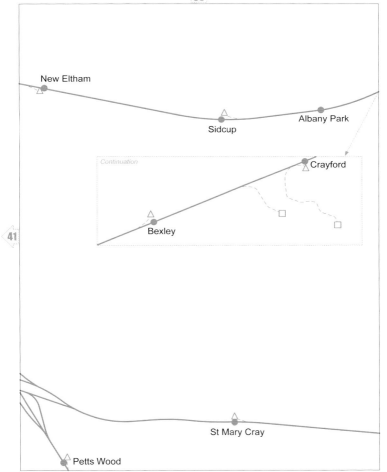

New Eltham

Sidcup

Albany Park

Continuation

Crayford

Bexley

St Mary Cray

Petts Wood

41

42

Scale

| Km | 0.5 | 1 | 1.5 | 2 |

| Miles | ¼ | ½ | ¾ | 1 |

0

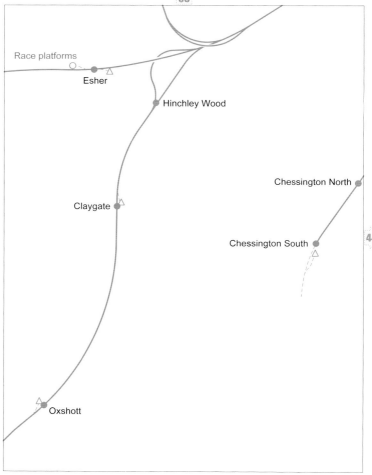

Race platforms

Esher

Hinchley Wood

Chessington North

Claygate

Chessington South

Oxshott

43

Scale

Km 0.5 1 1.5 2
0

Miles ¼ ½ ¾ 1

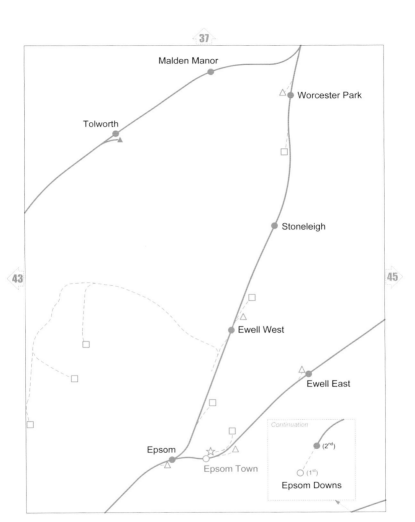

Malden Manor

Worcester Park

Tolworth

Stoneleigh

Ewell West

Ewell East

Continuation

Epsom

Epsom Town

(2nd)

(1st)

Epsom Downs

44

Scale

Km   0.5   1   1.5   2
0

Miles ¼   ½   ¾   1

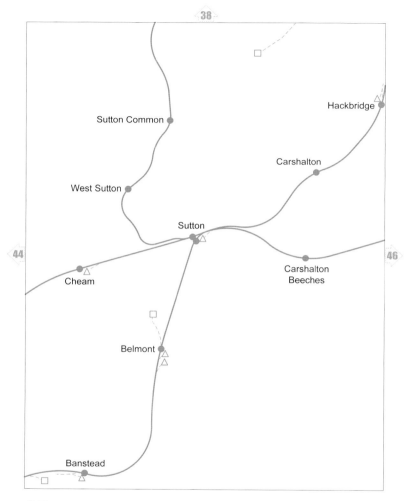

Sutton Common

Hackbridge

Carshalton

West Sutton

Sutton

Cheam

Carshalton
Beeches

Belmont

Banstead

45

Scale

Km 0.5 1 1.5 2
0

Miles ¼ ½ ¾ 1

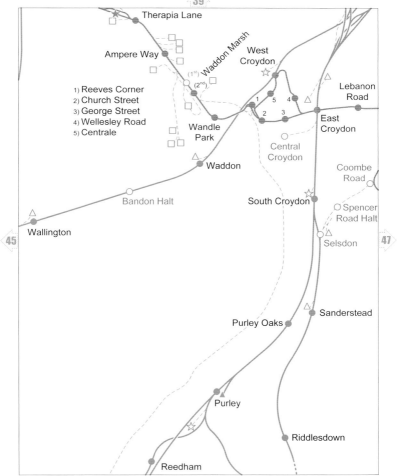

Therapia Lane

Ampere Way

(1ˢᵗ)
(2ⁿᵈ)

Waddon Marsh

West
Croydon

Lebanon
Road

1) Reeves Corner
2) Church Street
3) George Street
4) Wellesley Road
5) Centrale

1   5   4
2   3

East
Croydon

Wandle
Park

Central
Croydon

Coombe
Road

Waddon

Bandon Halt

South Croydon

Spencer
Road Halt

45

Wallington

Selsdon

47

Sanderstead

Purley Oaks

Purley

Riddlesdown

Reedham

46

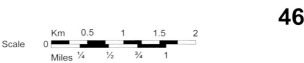

Scale Km 0   0.5   1   1.5   2

Miles ¼   ½   ¾   1

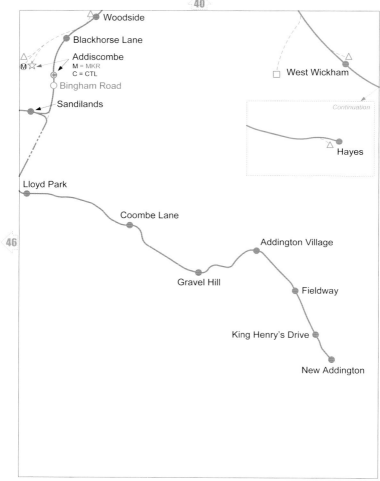

Woodside

Blackhorse Lane

Addiscombe
M = MKR
C = CTL

Bingham Road

Sandilands

West Wickham

Continuation

Hayes

Lloyd Park

Coombe Lane

Addington Village

Gravel Hill

Fieldway

King Henry's Drive

New Addington

47

Scale

Km   0.5   1   1.5   2
0
Miles ¼   ½   ¾   1

Index

Names quoted are the current names or the name at the point of closure. If two stations shared the same name, they are differentiated through the addition of the abbreviated railway company name that opened that station in brackets. Where more than one station shared the same name and were built by the same railway company, they are differentiated chronologically through the suffix (1st), (2nd), etc. Entries in black text denote open passenger stations, red closed, blue under construction or proposed (2015). Opening dates are usually the first full day of normal service, closure dates are the first full traffic day without trains. Some stations (e.g. Dalston Junction, Homerton, Shepherds Bush [WLR]) were closed for long periods of their existence, but as they were ultimately rebuilt on the same site, the original opening date is given.

A

Name	Page	Date opened	Date closed
Abbey Road	22	31/08/2011	N/A
Abbey Wood	33	??/??/1849	N/A
Acton Central	28	01/08/1853	N/A
Acton Main Line	18	01/02/1868	N/A
Acton Town	28	01/07/1879	N/A
Addington Village	47	10/05/2000	N/A
Addiscombe (MKR)	47	01/04/1864	02/06/1997
Addiscombe (CTL)	47	23/05/2000	N/A
Albany Park	42	07/07/1935	N/A
Aldgate	21	18/11/1876	N/A
Aldgate East	21	06/10/1884	N/A
Aldwych	20	30/11/1907	30/09/1994
Alexandra Palace (GNR)	11	01/05/1859	N/A
Alexandra Palace (MHPR)	11	24/05/1873	05/07/1954
All Saints (formerly Poplar [NLR] 01/08/1866 – 15/05/1944)	21	31/08/1987	N/A
Alperton	17	28/06/1903	N/A
Amersham	1	01/09/1892	N/A
Ampere Way	46	10/05/2000	N/A

Name	Page	Date opened	Date closed
Anerley	40	05/06/1839	N/A
Angel	20	17/11/1901	N/A
Angel Road	12	15/09/1840	N/A
Archway	20	22/06/1907	N/A
Arena	40	23/05/2000	N/A
Arnos Grove	11	19/09/1932	N/A
Arsenal	20	15/12/1906	N/A
Avenue Road	40	23/05/2000	N/A

B

Name	Page	Date opened	Date closed
Baker Street	19	10/01/1863	N/A
Balham	39	01/12/1856	N/A
Bandon Halt	46	11/06/1906	07/06/1914
Bank	20	08/08/1898	N/A
Banstead	45	22/05/1865	N/A
Barbican	20	23/12/1865	N/A
Barking	23	13/04/1854	N/A
Barking Riverside	23	TBA	N/A
Barkingside	14	01/05/1903	N/A
Barnehurst	34	01/05/1895	N/A
Barnes	28	27/07/1846	N/A
Barnes Bridge	28	12/03/1916	N/A
Barons Court	29	09/10/1905	N/A
Bath Road	28	08/04/1909	01/01/1917
Battersea (LUL)	30	c.2020	N/A
Battersea (WLER)	29	02/03/1863	21/10/1940
Battersea Park (1st)	30	01/10/1860	01/11/1870
Battersea Park (2nd)	30	01/05/1867	N/A
Battersea Park Road	30	01/05/1867	03/04/1916
Bayswater	19	01/10/1868	N/A
Beckenham Hill	40	01/07/1892	N/A
Beckenham Junction	40	01/01/1857	N/A
Beckenham Road	40	23/05/2000	N/A
Beckton (GCC)	23	17/03/1873	29/12/1940
Beckton (DLR)	22	28/03/1994	N/A

Name	Page	Date opened	Date closed
Beckton Park	32	28/03/1994	N/A
Becontree	23	28/06/1926	N/A
Beddington Lane	39	22/10/1855	N/A
Belgrave Walk	38	30/05/2000	N/A
Bellingham	40	01/07/1892	N/A
Belmont (LMS)	8	12/09/1932	05/10/1964
Belmont (LBSCR)	45	22/05/1865	N/A
Belsize Park	19	22/06/1907	N/A
Belvedere	34	??/03/1859	N/A
Bermondsey	31	17/09/1999	N/A
Bermondsey Street	30	10/10/1836	14/12/1836
Berrylands	37	16/10/1933	N/A
Bethnal Green (GER)	21	24/05/1872	N/A
Bethnal Green (LPTB)	21	04/12/1946	N/A
Bexley	42	01/09/1866	N/A
Bexleyheath	33	01/05/1895	N/A
Bickley	41	05/07/1858	N/A
Bingham Road	47	01/09/1906	16/05/1983
Birkbeck	40	02/03/1930	N/A
Bishopsgate (High Level)	21	01/07/1840	c.1879
Bishopsgate (Low Level)	21	04/11/1872	22/05/1916
Blackfriars (MDR)	20	30/05/1870	N/A
Blackfriars (SER)	30	11/01/1864	01/01/1869
Blackfriars Bridge	30	01/06/1864	01/10/1885
Blackheath	32	30/07/1849	N/A
Blackheath Hill	31	18/09/1871	01/01/1917
Blackhorse Lane	47	23/05/2000	N/A
Blackhorse Road	12	09/07/1894	N/A
Blackwall (DLR)	31	28/03/1994	N/A
Blackwall (LBLR)	32	06/07/1840	04/05/1926
Blake Hall	6	24/04/1865	31/10/1981
Bond Street (CLR)	20	24/09/1900	N/A
Bond Street (NR)	20	??/??/2018	N/A
Borough	30	18/12/1890	N/A
Borough Road	30	01/06/1864	01/04/1907

Name	Page	Date opened	Date closed
Boston Manor	27	01/05/1883	N/A
Bounds Green	11	19/09/1932	N/A
Bow	21	26/09/1850	15/05/1944
Bow Church	21	31/08/1987	N/A
Bow Road (LBLR)	21	02/04/1849	07/11/1949
Bow Road (MDR)	21	11/06/1902	N/A
Bowes Park	11	01/11/1880	N/A
Brent Cross	10	19/11/1923	N/A
Brent Cross Thameslink	9	TBA	N/A
Brentford (GWR)	27	01/05/1860	04/05/1942
Brentford (LSWR)	27	22/08/1849	N/A
Brentham for North Ealing and Greystoke Park	18	01/05/1911	15/06/1947
Brimsdown	5	01/10/1884	N/A
British Museum	20	30/07/1900	24/09/1933
Brixton (LCDR)	30	06/10/1862	N/A
Brixton (LTE)	30	23/07/1971	N/A
Broad Street	20	01/11/1865	30/06/1986
Brockley	31	06/03/1871	N/A
Brockley Lane	31	??/06/1872	01/01/1917
Bromley-By-Bow	21	31/03/1858	N/A
Bromley North	41	01/01/1878	N/A
Bromley South	41	22/11/1858	N/A
Brompton Road	29	15/12/1906	30/07/1934
Brondesbury	19	02/01/1860	N/A
Brondesbury Park	19	01/06/1908	N/A
Bruce Grove	12	22/07/1872	N/A
Buckhurst Hill	13	22/08/1856	N/A
Burdett Road	21	11/09/1871	21/04/1941
Burnt Oak	9	27/10/1924	N/A
Bushey	2	01/12/1841	N/A
Bush Hill Park	5	01/11/1880	N/A

C

Caledonian Road	20	15/12/1906	N/A

Name	Page	Date opened	Date closed
Caledonian Road & Barnsbury	20	10/06/1852	N/A
Camberwell	30	06/10/1862	03/04/1916
Cambridge Heath	21	27/05/1872	N/A
Camden Road (MID)	20	13/07/1868	01/01/1916
Camden Road (NLR)	20	07/12/1850	N/A
Camden Town	20	22/06/1907	N/A
Canada Water	31	19/08/1999	N/A
Canary Wharf (DLR)	31	12/08/1991	N/A
Canary Wharf (LUL)	31	17/09/1999	N/A
Canary Wharf (NR)	31	??/??/2018	N/A
Canning Town	22	14/06/1847	N/A
Cannon Street	20	01/09/1866	N/A
Cannon Street Road	21	21/08/1842	??/12/1848
Canonbury	20	01/09/1858	N/A
Canons Park	9	10/12/1932	N/A
Carpenders Park	7	01/04/1914	N/A
Carshalton	45	01/10/1868	N/A
Carshalton Beeches	45	01/10/1906	N/A
Carterhatch Lane	5	12/06/1916	01/07/1919
Cassiobridge	2	??/??/2017	N/A
Castle Bar Park	17	01/05/1904	N/A
Catford	40	01/07/1892	N/A
Catford Bridge	40	01/01/1857	N/A
Central	32	03/08/1880	09/09/1940
Central Croydon	46	01/01/1868	01/09/1890
Centrale	46	10/12/2005	N/A
Chadwell Heath	23	11/01/1864	N/A
Chalfont & Latimer	1	08/07/1889	N/A
Chalk Farm (UERL)	19	22/06/1907	N/A
Chalk Farm (LNWR)	19	01/11/1851	10/05/1915
Chancery Lane	20	30/07/1900	N/A
Charing Cross	30	11/01/1864	N/A
Charlton	32	30/07/1849	N/A
Cheam	45	10/05/1847	N/A
Chelsea & Fulham	29	02/03/1863	14/09/1940

Name	Page	Date opened	Date closed
Chesham	1	08/07/1889	N/A
Cheshunt	5	22/11/1841	N/A
Chessington North	43	28/05/1939	N/A
Chessington South	43	28/05/1939	N/A
Chigwell	14	01/05/1903	N/A
Chingford (1st)	13	17/11/1873	02/09/1878
Chingford (2nd)	6	02/09/1878	N/A
Chislehurst	41	01/07/1865	N/A
Chiswick	28	22/08/1849	N/A
Chiswick Park	28	01/07/1879	N/A
Chorleywood	1	08/07/1889	N/A
Church Manor Way Halt	33	01/01/1917	01/01/1920
Church Street	46	10/05/2000	N/A
City Road	20	17/11/1901	09/08/1922
City Thameslink	20	29/05/1990	N/A
Clapham Common (LSWR)	29	21/05/1838	02/03/1863
Clapham Common (CSLR)	30	03/06/1900	N/A
Clapham High Street	30	25/08/1862	N/A
Clapham Junction	29	02/03/1863	N/A
Clapham North	30	03/06/1900	N/A
Clapham South	30	13/09/1926	N/A
Clapton	21	01/07/1872	N/A
Claygate	43	02/02/1885	N/A
Clock House	40	01/05/1890	N/A
Coborn Road	21	01/02/1865	08/12/1946
Cockfosters	4	31/07/1933	N/A
Colindale	9	18/08/1924	N/A
Colliers Wood	38	13/08/1926	N/A
Colnbrook	25	09/08/1884	29/03/1965
Colnbrook Estate Halt	25	01/05/1961	29/03/1965
Colney Hatch Cemetery	11	10/07/1861	03/04/1863
Commercial Docks	31	01/05/1856	01/01/1867
Connaught Road	32	03/08/1880	08/09/1940
Coombe Lane	47	10/05/2000	N/A
Coombe Road	46	10/08/1885	16/05/1983

Name	Page	Date opened	Date closed
Covent Garden	20	11/04/1907	N/A
Cowley	15	01/10/1904	10/09/1962
Cranley Gardens	11	02/08/1902	05/07/1954
Crayford	42	01/09/1866	N/A
Crews Hill	4	04/04/1910	N/A
Cricklewood	19	02/05/1870	N/A
Crofton Park	31	01/07/1892	N/A
Crossharbour (formerly Millwall Docks 18/12/1871 – 04/05/1926)	31	31/08/1987	N/A
Crouch End	11	22/08/1867	05/07/1954
Crouch Hill	11	21/07/1868	N/A
Croxley	2	02/11/1925	N/A
Croxley Green	2	15/06/1912	25/03/1996
Crystal Palace	40	10/06/1854	N/A
Crystal Palace High Level	40	01/08/1865	20/09/1954
Custom House	32	26/11/1855	N/A
Cutty Sark	31	03/12/1999	N/A
Cyprus	32	28/03/1994	N/A

D

Name	Page	Date opened	Date closed
Dagenham Dock	24	01/07/1908	N/A
Dagenham East	24	01/05/1885	N/A
Dagenham Heathway	24	12/09/1932	N/A
Dalston Junction	21	01/11/1865	N/A
Dalston Kingsland	21	09/11/1850	N/A
Debden	6	24/04/1865	N/A
Denmark Hill	30	01/12/1865	N/A
Deptford	31	08/02/1836	N/A
Deptford Bridge	31	20/11/1999	N/A
Devonshire Street, Mile End	21	20/06/1839	c.1841
Devons Road	21	31/08/1987	N/A
Dollis Hill	18	01/10/1909	N/A
Down Street	30	15/03/1907	22/05/1932
Drayton Green	17	01/03/1905	N/A
Drayton Park	20	14/02/1904	N/A

Name	Page	Date opened	Date closed
Dudding Hill for Willesden & Neasden	18	03/08/1875	01/10/1902
Dundonald Road	38	30/05/2000	N/A

E

Name	Page	Date opened	Date closed
Ealing Broadway	17	01/12/1838	N/A
Ealing Common	28	01/07/1879	N/A
Earl's Court	29	30/10/1871	N/A
Earlsfield	38	01/04/1884	N/A
East Acton	18	03/08/1920	N/A
East Brixton	30	13/08/1866	05/01/1976
East Croydon	46	12/07/1841	N/A
East Dulwich	30	01/10/1868	N/A
East Finchley	10	22/08/1867	N/A
East Ham	22	31/03/1858	N/A
East India	32	28/03/1994	N/A
East Putney	29	03/06/1889	N/A
Eastcote	7	26/05/1906	N/A
Eden Park	40	29/05/1882	N/A
Edgware (GNR)	9	22/08/1867	11/09/1939
Edgware (UERL)	9	18/08/1924	N/A
Edgware Road (MET)	19	10/01/1863	N/A
Edgware Road (UERL)	19	15/06/1907	N/A
Edmonton Green	12	22/07/1872	N/A
Elephant & Castle	30	06/10/1862	N/A
Elm Park	24	13/05/1935	N/A
Elmers End	40	01/04/1864	N/A
Elmstead Woods	41	01/07/1904	N/A
Eltham	32	01/05/1895	N/A
Eltham Park	32	01/07/1908	17/03/1985
Elverson Road	31	20/11/1999	N/A
Embankment	30	30/05/1870	N/A
Emerson Park	24	01/10/1909	N/A
Enfield	4	01/04/1871	04/04/1910
Enfield Chase	4	04/04/1910	N/A

Name	Page	Date opened	Date closed
Enfield Lock	5	??/04/1855	N/A
Enfield Town	5	01/03/1849	N/A
Epping	6	24/04/1865	N/A
Epping Glade	6	N/A	N/A
Epsom	44	01/02/1859	N/A
Epsom Downs	44	22/05/1865	N/A
Epsom Town	44	10/05/1847	03/03/1929
Erith	34	30/07/1849	N/A
Esher	43	21/05/1838	N/A
Essex Road	20	14/02/1904	N/A
Euston	20	20/07/1837	N/A
Euston Square	20	10/01/1863	N/A
Ewell East	44	10/05/1847	N/A
Ewell West	44	04/04/1859	N/A

F

Name	Page	Date opened	Date closed
Fairlop	14	01/05/1903	N/A
Falconwood	33	01/01/1936	N/A
Farringdon	20	23/12/1865	N/A
Farringdon Street	20	10/01/1863	01/03/1866
Feltham	35	22/08/1848	N/A
Fenchurch Street	21	29/07/1841	N/A
Fieldway	47	10/05/2000	N/A
Finchley Central	10	22/08/1867	N/A
Finchley Road (MID)	19	13/07/1868	11/07/1927
Finchley Road (MSJWR)	19	30/06/1879	N/A
Finchley Road & Frognal	19	02/01/1860	N/A
Finsbury Park	20	01/07/1861	N/A
Forest Gate	22	??/??/1840	N/A
Forest Hill	40	05/06/1839	N/A
Fulham Broadway	29	01/03/1880	N/A
Fulwell	36	01/11/1864	N/A

Name	Page	Date opened	Date closed
G			
Gallions	33	late 1880	09/09/1940
Gallions Reach	33	28/03/1994	N/A
Gants Hill	14	14/12/1947	N/A
Garston	2	07/02/1966	N/A
George Street	46	10/05/2000	N/A
Gipsy Hill	39	01/12/1856	N/A
Globe Road & Devonshire Street	21	01/07/1884	22/05/1916
Gloucester Road	29	01/10/1868	N/A
Golders Green	10	22/06/1907	N/A
Goldhawk Road	28	01/04/1914	N/A
Goodge Street	20	22/06/1907	N/A
Goodmayes	23	08/02/1901	N/A
Gordon Hill	4	04/04/1910	N/A
Gospel Oak	20	02/01/1860	N/A
Grange Hill	14	01/05/1903	N/A
Grange Park	4	04/04/1910	N/A
Gravel Hill	47	10/05/2000	N/A
Great Portland Street	20	10/01/1863	N/A
Green Park	30	15/12/1906	N/A
Greenford (GWR)	17	01/10/1904	17/06/1963
Greenford (LPTB)	17	30/06/1947	N/A
Greenwich	31	24/12/1838	N/A
Greenwich Park	31	01/10/1888	01/01/1917
Grosvenor Road	30	01/11/1867	01/10/1911
Grove Park	41	01/11/1871	N/A
Gunnersbury	28	01/01/1869	N/A
H			
Hackbridge	45	01/10/1868	N/A
Hackney Central	21	26/09/1850	N/A
Hackney Downs	21	27/05/1872	N/A
Hackney Wick	21	12/05/1980	N/A
Hadley Wood	3	01/05/1885	N/A
Haggerston (NLR)	21	02/09/1867	06/05/1940

Name	Page	Date opened	Date closed
Haggerston (TFL)	21	27/04/2010	N/A
Hainault	14	01/05/1903	N/A
Hammersmith (MDR)	29	09/09/1874	N/A
Hammersmith (MET / GWR)	29	13/06/1864	N/A
Hammersmith & Chiswick	28	08/04/1858	01/01/1917
Hammersmith (Grove Road)	28	01/01/1869	05/06/1916
Hampstead	19	22/06/1907	N/A
Hampstead Heath	19	02/01/1860	N/A
Hampstead Road	20	09/06/1851	05/05/1855
Hampton	35	01/11/1864	N/A
Hampton Court	36	01/02/1849	N/A
Hampton Wick	36	01/07/1863	N/A
Hanger Lane	18	30/07/1947	N/A
Hanwell	17	01/12/1838	N/A
Harlesden	18	15/06/1912	N/A
Harlesden For West Willesden & Stonebridge Park	18	03/08/1875	01/10/1902
Harringay	11	01/05/1885	N/A
Harringay Green Lanes	11	01/06/1880	N/A
Harrington Road	40	23/05/2000	N/A
Harrow-On-The-Hill	8	02/08/1880	N/A
Harrow & Wealdstone	8	20/07/1837	N/A
Hatch End	8	08/08/1842	N/A
Hatton Cross	26	19/07/1975	N/A
Haverstock Hill	19	13/07/1868	01/01/1916
Haydons Road	38	01/10/1868	N/A
Hayes	47	29/05/1882	N/A
Hayes & Harlington	26	01/05/1864	N/A
Headstone Lane	8	10/02/1913	N/A
Heathrow Junction	25	19/01/1998	25/05/1998
Heathrow Terminals 1, 2 & 3	25	16/12/1977	N/A
Heathrow Terminal 4	25	12/04/1986	N/A
Heathrow Terminal 5	25	27/03/2008	N/A
Hendon	9	13/07/1868	N/A
Hendon Central	9	19/11/1923	N/A

Name	Page	Date opened	Date closed
Hendon Factory Platform	9	19/05/1918	??/??/1919
Herne Hill	30	25/08/1862	N/A
Heron Quays	31	31/08/1987	N/A
High Barnet	3	01/04/1872	N/A
High Street Kensington	29	01/10/1868	N/A
Highams Park	13	17/11/1873	N/A
Highbury & Islington	20	26/09/1850	N/A
Highgate (GNR)	11	22/08/1867	05/07/1954
Highgate (LPTB)	11	19/01/1941	N/A
Highgate Road High Level	20	21/07/1868	01/03/1918
Highgate Road Low Level	20	17/12/1900	01/03/1918
Hillingdon	15	10/12/1923	N/A
Hinchley Wood	43	20/10/1930	N/A
Hither Green	32	01/06/1895	N/A
Holborn	20	15/12/1906	N/A
Holborn Viaduct	20	02/03/1874	29/01/1990
Holborn Viaduct (Low Level)	20	01/08/1874	01/06/1916
Holland Park	29	30/07/1900	N/A
Holloway & Caledonian Road	20	??/??/1852	01/10/1915
Holloway Road	20	15/12/1906	N/A
Homerton	21	01/10/1868	N/A
Honor Oak	31	01/12/1865	20/09/1954
Honor Oak Park	31	01/04/1886	N/A
Hornchurch	24	01/05/1885	N/A
Hornsey	11	07/08/1850	N/A
Hornsey Road	20	01/01/1872	03/05/1943
Hounslow	27	01/02/1850	N/A
Hounslow Central	27	01/04/1886	N/A
Hounslow East	27	02/05/1909	N/A
Hounslow Town	27	01/05/1883	02/05/1909
Hounslow West	26	21/07/1884	N/A
Hoxton	21	27/04/2010	N/A
Hyde Park Corner	30	15/12/1906	N/A

Name	Page	Date opened	Date closed
I J			
Ickenham	16	25/09/1905	N/A
Ilford	23	20/06/1839	N/A
Imperial Wharf	29	27/09/2009	N/A
Island Gardens	31	31/08/1987	N/A
Isleworth	27	01/02/1850	N/A
Iver	25	01/12/1924	N/A
Junction Road	20	01/01/1872	03/05/1943
K			
Kempton Park	35	18/07/1878	N/A
Kennington	30	18/12/1890	N/A
Kensal Green	19	01/10/1916	N/A
Kensal Green & Harlesden	18	01/11/1861	01/07/1873
Kensal Rise	19	01/07/1873	N/A
Kensington (Olympia)	29	27/05/1844	N/A
Kent House	40	01/10/1884	N/A
Kentish Town	20	13/07/1868	N/A
Kentish Town West	20	01/04/1867	N/A
Kenton	8	15/06/1912	N/A
Kew	28	01/08/1853	01/02/1862
Kew Bridge	28	22/08/1849	N/A
Kew Gardens	28	01/01/1869	N/A
Kidbrooke	32	01/05/1895	N/A
Kilburn	19	24/11/1879	N/A
Kilburn High Road	19	c.1851/1852	N/A
Kilburn Park	19	31/01/1915	N/A
King George V	32	02/12/2005	N/A
King Henry's Drive	47	10/05/2000	N/A
King William Street	20	18/12/1890	25/02/1900
King's Cross	20	14/10/1852	N/A
King's Cross St Pancras	20	15/12/1906	N/A
King's Cross Thameslink	20	10/01/1863	09/12/2007
Kingsbury	9	10/12/1932	N/A
Kingston (1st)	37	21/05/1838	??/??/1845

Name	Page	Date opened	Date closed
Kingston (2nd)	36	01/07/1863	N/A
Knightsbridge	29	15/12/1906	N/A

L

Name	Page	Date opened	Date closed
Ladbroke Grove	19	13/06/1864	N/A
Ladywell	31	01/01/1857	N/A
Lambeth North	30	10/03/1906	N/A
Lancaster Gate	19	30/07/1900	N/A
Langdon Park	21	10/12/2007	N/A
Latimer Road	19	16/12/1868	N/A
Lea Bridge (closed 08/07/1985 but to re-open December 2015)	21	15/09/1840	08/07/1985
Lebanon Road	46	10/05/2000	N/A
Lee	32	01/09/1866	N/A
Leicester Square	20	15/12/1906	N/A
Leman Street	21	01/06/1877	07/07/1941
Lewisham	31	30/07/1849	N/A
Lewisham Road	31	18/09/1871	01/01/1917
Leyton	22	22/08/1856	N/A
Leyton Midland Road	21	09/07/1894	N/A
Leytonstone	22	22/08/1856	N/A
Leytonstone High Road	22	09/07/1894	N/A
Limehouse (1st)	21	06/07/1840	04/05/1926
Limehouse (2nd)	21	03/08/1840	N/A
Liverpool Street	20	02/02/1874	N/A
Lloyd Park	47	10/05/2000	N/A
London Bridge	30	14/12/1836	N/A
London City Airport	32	02/12/2005	N/A
London Fields	21	27/05/1872	N/A
Lord's	19	13/04/1868	20/11/1939
Lordship Lane	40	01/09/1865	20/09/1954
Loughborough Junction	30	??/10/1864	N/A
Loughton (ECR)	6	22/08/1856	24/04/1865
Loughton (GER)	6	24/04/1865	N/A
Lower Edmonton (Low Level)	12	01/03/1849	11/09/1939

Name	Page	Date opened	Date closed
Lower Sydenham	40	01/01/1857	N/A
Ludgate Hill	20	21/12/1864	02/03/1929

M

Name	Page	Date opened	Date closed
Maida Vale	19	06/06/1915	N/A
Maiden Lane (GNR)	20	07/08/1850	14/10/1852
Maiden Lane (NLR)	20	01/07/1887	01/01/1917
Malden Manor	44	29/05/1938	N/A
Manor House	11	19/09/1932	N/A
Manor Park	22	06/01/1873	N/A
Manor Way	33	??//07/1881	09/09/1940
Mansion House	20	03/07/1871	N/A
Marble Arch	19	30/07/1900	N/A
Marlborough Road	19	13/04/1868	20/11/1939
Maryland	22	06/01/1873	N/A
Marylebone	19	15/03/1899	N/A
Maze Hill	32	01/01/1873	N/A
Merton Abbey	38	01/10/1868	03/03/1929
Merton Park	38	01/10/1868	N/A
Mildmay Park	20	01/01/1880	01/10/1934
Mile End (ECR)	21	c.1841	24/05/1872
Mile End (MDR)	21	02/06/1902	N/A
Mill Hill Broadway	9	13/07/1868	N/A
Mill Hill East	10	22/08/1867	N/A
Mill Hill (The Hale)	9	11/06/1906	11/09/1939
Millwall Junction	31	18/12/1871	04/05/1926
Minories	21	06/07/1840	24/10/1853
Mitcham	38	22/10/1855	N/A
Mitcham Eastfields	38	02/06/2008	N/A
Mitcham Junction	38	01/10/1868	N/A
Mitre Bridge Exchange Platforms	18	27/05/1844	01/12/1844
Monument	20	06/10/1884	N/A
Moor Park	7	09/05/1910	N/A
Moorgate	20	23/12/1865	N/A
Morden	38	13/09/1926	N/A

Name	Page	Date opened	Date closed
Morden Road	38	??/03/1857	N/A
Morden South	38	05/01/1930	N/A
Mornington Crescent	20	22/06/1907	N/A
Mortlake	28	27/07/1846	N/A
Motspur Park	37	12/07/1925	N/A
Mottingham	41	01/09/1866	N/A
Mudchute	31	31/08/1987	N/A
Muswell Hill	11	24/05/1873	05/07/1954

N

Name	Page	Date opened	Date closed
Neasden	18	02/08/1880	N/A
Necropolis	30	13/11/1854	11/05/1941
New Addington	47	10/05/2000	N/A
New Barnet	3	07/08/1850	N/A
New Beckenham	40	01/04/1864	N/A
New Cross (SER)	31	??/10/1850	N/A
New Cross (ELR)	31	07/12/1869	01/09/1886
New Cross Gate	31	05/06/1839	N/A
New Eltham	42	01/04/1878	N/A
New Malden	37	??/12/1846	N/A
New Southgate	11	07/08/1850	N/A
New Wandsworth	29	29/03/1858	01/11/1869
Newbury Park	14	01/05/1903	N/A
Nine Elms (LSWR)	30	21/05/1838	11/07/1848
Nine Elms (LUL)	30	??/??/2020	N/A
Nine Elms Royal Station	30	??/??/1854	??/??/1876
Noel Park & Wood Green	11	01/01/1878	07/01/1963
Norbiton	37	01/01/1869	N/A
Norbury	39	01/01/1878	N/A
North Acton	18	05/11/1923	N/A
North Acton Halt	18	01/05/1904	01/02/1913
North Dulwich	30	01/10/1868	N/A
North Ealing	18	23/06/1903	N/A
North End (or Bull & Bush)	19	N/A	N/A
North Greenwich (LUL)	32	14/05/1999	N/A

Name	Page	Date opened	Date closed
North Greenwich (MER)	31	29/07/1872	04/05/1926
North Harrow	8	22/03/1915	N/A
North Sheen	28	06/07/1930	N/A
North Weald	6	24/04/1865	N/A
North Wembley	17	15/06/1912	N/A
North Woolwich	32	14/06/1847	10/12/2006
Northfields	27	16/04/1908	N/A
Northolt (GWR)	17	01/05/1907	21/11/1948
Northolt (LTE)	17	21/11/1948	N/A
Northolt Park	17	19/07/1926	N/A
Northumberland Park	12	01/04/1842	N/A
Northwick Park	8	28/06/1923	N/A
Northwood	7	01/09/1887	N/A
Northwood Hills	7	13/11/1933	N/A
Norwood Junction	40	05/06/1839	N/A
Notting Hill Gate	29	01/10/1868	N/A
Nunhead	31	18/09/1871	N/A

O

Name	Page	Date opened	Date closed
Oakleigh Park	3	01/12/1873	N/A
Oakwood	4	13/03/1933	N/A
Old Ford	21	01/07/1867	N/A
Old Kent Road & Hatcham	31	13/08/1866	01/01/1917
Old Oak Lane Halt	18	01/10/1906	30/06/1947
Old Street	20	17/11/1901	N/A
Ongar	6	24/04/1865	N/A
Osterley	27	01/05/1883	N/A
Oval	30	18/12/1890	N/A
Oxford Circus	20	30/07/1900	N/A
Oxshott	43	02/02/1885	N/A

P

Name	Page	Date opened	Date closed
Paddington (1st)	19	04/06/1838	29/05/1854
Paddington (2nd)	19	16/01/1854	N/A
Palace Gates Wood Green	11	07/10/1878	07/01/1963

Name	Page	Date opened	Date closed
Palmers Green	11	01/04/1871	N/A
Park Royal (GWR)	18	15/06/1903	27/09/1937
Park Royal (UERL)	18	06/07/1931	N/A
Park Royal & Twyford Abbey	18	23/06/1903	06/07/1931
Park Royal West Halt	18	20/06/1932	15/06/1947
Parsons Green	29	01/03/1880	N/A
Peckham Rye	31	01/12/1865	N/A
Penge	40	03/05/1858	c.1860
Penge East	40	01/07/1863	N/A
Penge West	40	05/06/1839	N/A
Perivale (GWR)	17	01/05/1904	15/06/1947
Perivale (LPTB)	17	30/06/1947	N/A
Petts Wood	42	09/07/1928	N/A
Phipps Bridge	38	30/05/2000	N/A
Piccadilly Circus	20	10/03/1906	N/A
Pimlico (LTE)	30	14/09/1972	N/A
Pimlico (WELCPR)	30	29/03/1858	01/10/1860
Pinner	7	25/05/1885	N/A
Plaistow	22	31/03/1858	N/A
Plumstead	33	16/07/1859	N/A
Ponders End	5	15/09/1840	N/A
Pontoon Dock	32	02/12/2005	N/A
Poplar (LBLR)	32	06/07/1840	04/05/1926
Poplar (EWIDBJR - did not open)	31	N/A	N/A
Poplar (DLR)	31	31/08/1987	N/A
Poyle Estate Halt	25	04/01/1954	29/03/1965
Poyle For Stanwell Moor Halt	25	01/06/1927	29/03/1965
Preston Road	9	21/05/1908	N/A
Primrose Hill	19	05/05/1855	23/09/1992
Prince Regent	32	28/03/1994	N/A
Pudding Mill Lane	21	15/01/1996	N/A
Purley	46	12/07/1841	N/A
Purley Oaks	46	05/11/1899	N/A
Putney	29	27/07/1846	N/A
Putney Bridge	29	01/03/1880	N/A

Name	Page	Date opened	Date closed
Q			
Queens Park	19	02/06/1879	N/A
Queen's Road	21	N/A	N/A
Queens Road Peckham	31	13/08/1866	N/A
Queenstown Road Battersea	30	01/11/1877	N/A
Queensbury	9	16/12/1934	N/A
Queensway	19	30/07/1900	N/A
R			
Rainham	24	13/04/1854	N/A
Ravensbourne	41	01/07/1892	N/A
Ravenscourt Park	28	01/04/1873	N/A
Rayners Lane	7	26/05/1906	N/A
Raynes Park	37	30/10/1871	N/A
Rectory Road	21	27/05/1872	N/A
Redbridge	13	14/12/1947	N/A
Reedham	46	01/03/1911	N/A
Reeves Corner	46	10/05/2000	N/A
Regent's Park	20	10/03/1906	N/A
Richmond	27	27/07/1846	N/A
Rickmansworth	1	01/09/1887	N/A
Rickmansworth (Church Street)	1	01/10/1862	03/03/1952
Riddlesdown	46	05/06/1927	N/A
Roding Valley	13	03/02/1936	N/A
Rotherhithe	31	07/12/1869	N/A
Royal Albert	32	28/03/1994	N/A
Royal Oak	19	30/10/1871	N/A
Royal Showground	18	23/06/1903	27/06/1903
Royal Victoria	32	28/03/1994	N/A
Rugby Road	28	08/04/1909	01/01/1917
Ruislip	7	04/07/1904	N/A
Ruislip Gardens	16	09/07/1934	N/A
Ruislip Manor	7	05/08/1912	N/A
Russell Square	20	15/12/1906	N/A

Name	Page	Date opened	Date closed
S			
St Ann's Road	11	02/10/1882	09/08/1942
St Helier	38	05/01/1930	N/A
St James's Park	30	24/12/1868	N/A
St James Street Walthamstow	12	26/04/1870	N/A
St Johns	31	01/06/1873	N/A
St John's Wood	19	20/11/1939	N/A
St Margarets	27	02/10/1876	N/A
St Mary Cray	41	03/12/1860	N/A
St Mary's (Whitechapel Road)	21	03/03/1884	01/05/1938
St Pancras International	20	01/10/1868	N/A
St Paul's	20	30/07/1900	N/A
St Quintin Park & Wormwood Scrubs	18	01/08/1871	03/10/1940
Sanderstead	46	10/03/1884	N/A
Sandilands	47	10/05/2000	N/A
Selhurst	39	01/05/1865	N/A
Selsdon	46	10/08/1885	16/05/1983
Seven Kings	23	01/03/1899	N/A
Seven Sisters	12	22/07/1872	N/A
Shadwell	21	01/10/1840	N/A
Shepherd's Bush (CLR)	29	30/07/1900	N/A
Shepherd's Bush (MET / GWR) (1st)	28	13/06/1864	01/04/1914
Shepherd's Bush (MET / GWR) (2nd)	29	01/07/1864	01/11/1869
Shepherd's Bush (LSWR)	29	01/05/1874	05/06/1916
Shepherd's Bush (WLR)	29	27/05/1844	N/A
Shepherd's Bush Market	28	01/04/1914	N/A
Shepperton	35	01/11/1864	N/A
Shern Hall Street, Walthamstow	12	26/04/1870	17/11/1873
Shoreditch (NLR)	21	01/11/1865	04/10/1940
Shoreditch (ELR)	21	10/04/1876	11/06/2006
Shoreditch High Street	21	27/04/2010	N/A
Shortlands	41	03/05/1858	N/A
Sidcup	42	01/09/1866	N/A
Silver Street	12	22/07/1872	N/A

Name	Page	Date opened	Date closed
Silvertown	32	19/06/1863	10/12/2006
Slade Green	34	01/07/1900	N/A
Sloane Square	29	24/12/1868	N/A
Smallberry Green	27	22/08/1849	01/02/1850
Snaresbrook	13	22/08/1856	N/A
South Acton	28	01/01/1880	N/A
South Bermondsey	31	13/08/1866	N/A
South Bromley	21	01/09/1884	15/05/1944
South Croydon	46	01/09/1865	N/A
South Dock	31	18/12/1871	04/05/1926
South Ealing	27	01/05/1883	N/A
South Greenford	17	20/09/1926	N/A
South Hampstead	19	02/06/1879	N/A
South Harrow	17	28/06/1903	N/A
South Kensington	29	24/12/1868	N/A
South Kentish Town	20	22/06/1907	05/06/1924
South Kenton	17	03/07/1933	N/A
South Merton	38	07/07/1929	N/A
South Quay	31	31/08/1987	N/A
South Ruislip	16	01/05/1908	N/A
South Tottenham	12	01/05/1871	N/A
South Wimbledon	38	13/09/1926	N/A
South Woodford	13	22/08/1856	N/A
Southall	26	01/05/1839	N/A
Southbury	5	01/10/1891	N/A
Southfields	38	03/06/1889	N/A
Southgate	4	13/03/1933	N/A
Southwark	30	20/11/1999	N/A
Southwark Park	31	01/10/1902	15/03/1915
Spa Road, Bermondsey	31	08/02/1836	15/03/1915
Spencer Road Halt	46	01/09/1906	15/03/1915
Stamford Brook	28	01/02/1912	N/A
Stamford Hill	12	22/07/1872	N/A
Stanmore	8	10/12/1932	N/A
Stanmore Village	8	18/12/1890	15/09/1952

Name	Page	Date opened	Date closed
Star Lane	22	31/08/2011	N/A
Stepney Green	21	23/06/1902	N/A
Stewarts Lane (LCDR)	30	01/05/1863	01/01/1867
Stewarts Lane (WELCPR)	30	29/03/1858	01/12/1858
Stoke Newington	21	27/05/1872	N/A
Stockwell	30	18/12/1890	N/A
Stonebridge Park	18	15/06/1912	N/A
Stoneleigh	44	17/07/1932	N/A
Stratford	22	20/06/1839	N/A
Stratford High Street (formerly Stratford Market 14/06/1847 – 06/05/1957)	22	31/08/2011	N/A
Stratford International	21	30/11/2009	N/A
Strawberry Hill	36	01/12/1873	N/A
Streatham	39	01/10/1868	N/A
Streatham Common	39	01/12/1862	N/A
Streatham Hill	39	01/12/1856	N/A
Stroud Green	11	11/04/1881	05/07/1954
Sudbury & Harrow Road	17	01/03/1906	N/A
Sudbury Hill	17	28/06/1903	N/A
Sudbury Hill Harrow	17	01/03/1906	N/A
Sudbury Town	17	28/06/1903	N/A
Sunbury	35	01/11/1864	N/A
Sundridge Park	41	01/01/1878	N/A
Surbiton	36	??/??/1845	N/A
Surrey Canal Road	31	TBA	N/A
Surrey Quays	31	07/12/1869	N/A
Sutton	45	10/05/1847	N/A
Sutton Common	45	05/01/1930	N/A
Swiss Cottage (MSJWR)	19	13/04/1868	18/08/1940
Swiss Cottage (LPTB)	19	20/11/1939	N/A
Sydenham	40	05/06/1839	N/A
Sydenham Hill	40	01/08/1863	N/A
Syon Lane	27	05/07/1931	N/A

Name	Page	Date opened	Date closed
T			
Teddington	36	01/07/1863	N/A
Temple	20	30/05/1870	N/A
Thames Ditton	36	??/11/1851	N/A
Thames Wharf	32	TBA	N/A
Theobalds Grove	5	01/10/1891	N/A
Therapia Lane	46	30/05/2000	N/A
Theydon Bois	6	24/04/1865	N/A
Thornton Heath	39	01/12/1862	N/A
Tidal Basin	32	??/02/1858	15/08/1943
Tolworth	44	29/05/1938	N/A
Tooting	38	01/10/1868	N/A
Tooting Bec	38	13/09/1926	N/A
Tooting Broadway	38	13/09/1926	N/A
Tottenham Court Road	20	30/07/1900	N/A
Tottenham Hale	12	15/09/1840	N/A
Totteridge & Whetstone	3	01/04/1872	N/A
Tower Gateway	21	31/08/1987	N/A
Tower Hill (MDR / MET)	21	06/10/1884	05/02/1967
Tower Hill (MET)	21	25/09/1882	N/A
Trumper's Crossing Halte	27	01/07/1904	01/02/1926
Tufnell Park	20	22/06/1907	N/A
Tulse Hill	39	01/10/1868	N/A
Turkey Street	5	01/10/1891	N/A
Turnham Green	28	01/01/1869	N/A
Turnpike Lane	11	19/09/1932	N/A
Twickenham	27	22/08/1848	N/A
Twyford Abbey Halt	18	01/05/1904	01/05/1911

Name	Page	Date opened	Date closed
U V			
Upminster	24	01/05/1885	N/A
Upminster Bridge	24	17/12/1934	N/A
Upney	23	12/09/1932	N/A
Upper Halliford	35	01/05/1944	N/A

Name	Page	Date opened	Date closed
Upper Holloway	20	21/07/1868	N/A
Upper Sydenham	40	01/08/1884	20/09/1954
Upton Park	22	17/09/1877	N/A
Uxbridge (1st)	15	04/07/1904	04/12/1938
Uxbridge (2nd)	15	04/12/1938	N/A
Uxbridge High Street	15	01/05/1907	01/09/1939
Uxbridge Road	29	01/11/1869	21/10/1940
Uxbridge Vine Street	15	08/09/1856	N/A
Vauxhall	30	11/07/1848	N/A
Victoria	30	01/10/1860	N/A
Victoria Park	21	14/06/1856	08/11/1943
Victoria Park & Bow	21	02/04/1849	06/01/1851

W Y

Name	Page	Date opened	Date closed
Waddon	46	??/02/1863	N/A
Waddon Marsh	46	06/07/1930	N/A
Wallington	46	10/05/1847	N/A
Waltham Cross	5	15/09/1840	N/A
Walthamstow Central	12	26/04/1870	N/A
Walthamstow Queen's Road	12	09/07/1894	N/A
Walworth Road	30	01/05/1863	03/04/1916
Wandle Park	46	30/05/2000	N/A
Wandsworth Common	38	01/12/1856	N/A
Wandsworth Road	30	01/03/1863	N/A
Wandsworth Town	29	27/07/1846	N/A
Wanstead	13	14/12/1947	N/A
Wanstead Park	22	09/07/1894	N/A
Wapping	31	07/12/1869	N/A
Warren Street	20	22/06/1907	N/A
Warwick Avenue	19	31/01/1915	N/A
Waterloo	30	11/07/1848	N/A
Waterloo East	30	01/01/1869	N/A
Watford	2	02/11/1925	??/??/2017
Watford High Street	2	01/10/1862	N/A
Watford Junction	2	20/07/1837	N/A

Name	Page	Date opened	Date closed
Watford North	2	01/10/1910	N/A
Watford Stadium	2	04/12/1982	14/05/1993
Watford Vicarage Road	2	??/??/2017	N/A
Watford West	2	15/06/1912	25/03/1996
Wellesley Road	46	10/05/2000	N/A
Welling	33	01/05/1895	N/A
Welsh Harp	9	02/05/1870	01/07/1903
Wembley Central	18	08/08/1842	N/A
Wembley Park	18	12/05/1894	N/A
Wembley Stadium (LNER)	18	28/04/1923	18/05/1968
Wembley Stadium (GCR)	18	01/03/1906	N/A
West Acton	18	05/11/1923	N/A
West Brompton	29	01/09/1866	N/A
West Croydon	46	05/06/1839	N/A
West Drayton	25	04/06/1838	N/A
West Dulwich	39	??/10/1863	N/A
West Ealing	17	01/03/1871	N/A
West Finchley	10	01/03/1933	N/A
West Green	11	01/01/1878	N/A
West Ham	22	01/02/1901	N/A
West Hampstead (MSJWR)	19	30/06/1879	N/A
West Hampstead (LNWR)	19	01/03/1888	N/A
West Hampstead Thameslink	19	01/03/1871	N/A
West Harrow	8	17/11/1913	N/A
West India Docks	31	06/07/1840	04/05/1926
West India Quay	31	31/08/1987	N/A
West Kensington	29	09/09/1874	N/A
West London Junction	18	27/05/1844	01/12/1844
West Norwood	39	01/12/1856	N/A
West Ruislip	16	02/04/1906	N/A
West Silvertown	32	02/12/2005	N/A
West Sutton	45	05/01/1930	N/A
West Wickham	47	29/05/1882	N/A
Westbourne Park	19	01/02/1866	N/A
Westcombe Park	32	01/05/1879	N/A

Name	Page	Date opened	Date closed
Westferry	31	31/08/1987	N/A
Westminster	30	24/12/1868	N/A
White City (LPTB)	19	23/11/1947	N/A
White City (MET / GWR)	29	01/05/1908	25/10/1959
White Hart Lane	12	22/07/1872	N/A
Whitechapel	21	10/04/1876	N/A
Whitton	27	06/07/1930	N/A
Willesden	18	early 1841	01/09/1866
Willesden Green	19	24/11/1879	N/A
Willesden Junction	18	01/09/1866	N/A
Wimbledon	38	21/05/1838	N/A
Wimbledon Chase	38	07/07/1929	N/A
Wimbledon Park	38	03/06/1889	N/A
Winchmore Hill	4	01/04/1871	N/A
Wood Green	11	19/09/1932	N/A
Wood Lane (CLR)	29	14/05/1908	23/11/1947
Wood Lane (LUL)	19	12/10/2008	N/A
Wood Street	13	17/11/1873	N/A
Woodford	13	22/08/1856	N/A
Woodgrange Park	22	09/07/1894	N/A
Woodside	47	??/07/1871	N/A
Woodside Park	10	01/04/1872	N/A
Woodstock Road	28	08/04/1909	01/01/1917
Woolwich	33	??/??/2018	N/A
Woolwich Arsenal	33	01/11/1849	N/A
Woolwich Dockyard	32	30/07/1849	N/A
Worcester Park	44	04/04/1859	N/A
York Road	20	15/12/1906	17/09/1932